for Prism
Premiered November 19, 2004 at Symphony Space, New

Scherzino

Baritone Saxophone in E♭

2004

*trattenuto = just slightly held back

Baritone Saxophone in E♭

Scherzino

WILLIAM BOLCOM

Baritone Saxophone in E♭